WHERE'S THE
Ballerina?

ILLUSTRATED BY
Abigail Goh

WRITTEN BY
Anna Claybourne

IVY KIDS

About
This Book

In this book, you can explore ten of the world's best-loved ballets.
There are tales packed with romance and betrayal,
magic and mystery, and excitement and celebration.

For each ballet, read the summary to help you understand
the story. You'll soon discover how the best ballets are full
of funny mix-ups, thrilling drama and, most importantly,
huge casts of wonderful characters in colourful costumes.

Then, turn the page and hunt for the characters hidden in
the busy ballet scene. Can you also spot the beautiful ballerina,
pictured below, in each scene? If you look very carefully,
you might find a peacock hidden in each picture, too...

Our
ballerina

THE Ballets

Swan Lake

Setting: Germany, long, long ago

Swan Lake is one of the most famous and the most romantic of all ballets.
Prince Siegfried is told that he has to get married, but how can he when he's never been
in love? Out in the forest one night, he finds a magical lake and a beautiful princess
called Odette. The Princess has been cursed and must live as a swan during the day, only
becoming human when the sun sets. Siegfried tries to free Odette from the terrible curse,
but an evil baron and his horrible daughter make things very difficult for him!

It's Prince Siegfried's 21st birthday. His mother gives him a crossbow as a present and tells him that he must find a wife at the party she is planning to throw the next night. Siegfried is very unhappy about this news, so he goes out hunting with his friends to cheer himself up.

Late at night, Siegfried gets lost in the forest alone. He finds an enchanted lake, where he sees something very strange – a swan wearing a crown. He is about to shoot the swan with his new crossbow, when it magically changes into a beautiful princess. At once, Siegfried falls head over heels in love.

The Swan Princess is called Odette. She says that the wicked Baron von Rothbart has cursed her and her friends to live at the magical lake as swans, only becoming humans when night falls. The evil spell can only be broken if someone swears to love her forever and keeps their promise to stay true to her.

The evil Baron appears as a giant owl and Siegfried tries to kill him, but Odette stops him, as she knows that then the curse would never end. Siegfried, madly in love with Odette, promises to be true to her forever. They dance together until the sun comes up, when she must become a swan again.

FIND THESE CHARACTERS OVER THE PAGE

Odette,
the Swan Princess

Prince
Siegfried

Prince
Siegfried's mother

Baron von
Rothbart

Odile, Rothbart's
daughter

Odette's
swan friends

At the party the next night, Siegfried meets many princesses, but he's not interested in any of them, as he only has eyes for Odette. Baron von Rothbart arrives in his human form with his evil daughter, Odile, who looks exactly like Odette. Siegfried thinks that she is Odette and happily announces that he wants to marry her.

To his horror, Siegfried then sees the real Odette. She has been watching through the window and is heartbroken. Siegfried hasn't kept his promise to be true to her forever, meaning that the Baron's evil curse can never be broken. Devastated by what he's done, Siegfried follows Odette back to the lake and begs her to forgive him, which she does.

Baron von Rothbart arrives at the lake with Odile, and tells Siegfried that he must marry her as he promised he would. Siegfried refuses and he and Odette throw themselves into the lake to drown together. The spell breaks and Odette's friends are set free from the curse. They then force the Baron and Odile towards the lake and under the water.

Romeo and Juliet

Setting: Verona, Italy, in medieval times

Romeo and Juliet is a ballet based on a very famous love story by William Shakespeare. Young Romeo and Juliet fall madly in love, but their families are enemies. The couple manage to marry in secret, but disaster strikes when Romeo is caught up in a street fight and is banished from the city. Meanwhile, Juliet's parents plan to marry her to another man. Things go from bad to worse as they try to be together against the odds. It ends very sadly…

In the market square, fighting breaks out between two enemy families, the Montagues and the Capulets. A local prince orders the fighting to stop, saying that anyone involved in future fights will be punished. Meanwhile, Lord and Lady Capulet are planning a grand ball, where they hope to find a husband for their teenage daughter, Juliet.

The next night, the Capulets' ball is in full swing, with delicious food, good music and lots of dancing. Romeo, the son of the Montague family, and his two friends Benvolio and Mercutio, sneak into the ball, even though Montagues are not welcome. There, Romeo meets Juliet, and they fall madly in love. Tybalt Capulet, Juliet's cousin, spots Romeo and is angry that he has come to the ball uninvited.

Later that night, Romeo finds Juliet on her balcony and they swear their love for each other. The next day, Juliet's nursemaid takes a message to Romeo asking him to meet Juliet at the home of Friar Laurence. The Friar secretly marries the happy couple, hoping that when their families find out about the wedding, they will end their bitter feud and the fighting will stop.

FIND THESE CHARACTERS OVER THE PAGE

The Prince

Mercutio

Tybalt

Romeo and Juliet

Paris

Friar
Laurence

Back in the market square, Romeo meets Tybalt, who wants to fight him for gatecrashing the Capulets' ball. Romeo refuses, so Tybalt fights Mercutio instead, and kills him. Furious at the death of his best friend, Romeo attacks and kills Tybalt in revenge. As punishment, Romeo must leave the city, but first he goes to see Juliet.

In the morning, Romeo and Juliet have to say goodbye to each other. Romeo then flees the city, leaving Juliet very upset. Juliet's mother and father tell her that she must marry a young man called Paris. Juliet is horrified; she is in love with Romeo and has already secretly married him. In desperation, she goes to see Friar Laurence to ask for help.

Friar Laurence gives Juliet a sleeping potion that will make it look as though she has died, so that she doesn't have to marry Paris. The Friar sends a message to Romeo explaining the plan and asking him to come back to Verona to rescue Juliet. But the message gets lost. Unaware of what's happened, Juliet drinks the potion. Her family find her in the morning and think she has died, so they place her in the family tomb.

Instead of getting the Friar's message, Romeo only hears that Juliet has died. Devastated by the news, he buys poison and goes to the Capulets' tomb. When he arrives, he finds Paris visiting Juliet's body, and he fights and kills him. Then he drinks the poison and lies down beside Juliet. She wakes up and finds Romeo dead. Realizing what's happened, she kills herself with his dagger.

Giselle

Setting: A German village, in medieval times

Set in Germany, *Giselle* is a romantic ballet about a peasant girl called Giselle and a local duke called Albrecht. The Duke pretends to be a young villager so that he can date Giselle and, to make things even more complicated, he's already engaged to someone else. The spooky tale that unfolds is one of disguises, ghosts and deadly dances. As you can imagine, it doesn't have a very happy ending.

Albrecht, a local duke, falls in love with a beautiful peasant girl called Giselle. So that he can date her, he disguises himself as a young villager called Loys and moves into a cottage near Giselle's house. Hilarion, a gamekeeper who also loves Giselle, tries to tell her that Loys is not what he seems, but Giselle ignores him and falls madly in love with Loys.

Not only is Albrecht secretly a duke, but he is also already engaged to be married to someone else – Princess Bathilde. Unaware of all of this, Giselle agrees to dance in the village to celebrate the grape harvest. Giselle's mother interrupts and tells her not to dance so much as she has a weak heart and it could be dangerous.

Giselle's mother warns Giselle that, if she is not careful, she will die and become a Wili. The Wilis are ghosts of young women who died before they got married. Every night at midnight, they rise from their graves and haunt the forest, dancing until the sun comes up. If a man passes by, they surround him and make him dance until he falls down dead.

A hunting party visits the village, and it includes Princess Bathilde. Albrecht hides because he doesn't want her to recognize him. Hilarion finds Albrecht's real clothes and royal hunting sword in his cottage, and tells Giselle who Albrecht really is. Giselle doesn't believe him, so Hilarion calls back the hunters. They recognize Albrecht and reveal his true identity.

FIND THESE CHARACTERS OVER THE PAGE

Giselle

Albrecht,
disguised as
Loys

Hilarion

Giselle's
mother

Myrtha, Queen
of the Wilis

Princess
Bathilde

When Giselle realizes that Loys is really Albrecht, and that he is engaged to Bathilde, she goes mad with grief and begins a terrifying dance. Everyone tries to stop her, but she dances so wildly that her weak heart gives up and she dies. She is buried in the forest, with only a simple cross to mark her grave.

Heartbroken, Hilarion goes to visit Giselle's grave. When it is nearly midnight, he remembers that the Wilis will soon appear and begin their deadly dance. He runs away, but the Wilis catch him and force him to dance until he dies. Myrtha, Queen of the Wilis, summons Giselle from her grave to become a Wili and dance with the others.

Devastated by Giselle's death, Albrecht arrives to bring flowers to her grave. He sees Giselle's ghost and follows her, but the other Wilis force him to dance until he is completely exhausted. Forgiving his betrayal, Giselle's ghost tries to save Albrecht by making him hold onto the cross on her grave, but Myrtha forces them away and the ghostly dance carries on. Albrecht almost dies, but as the sun begins to rise, the Wilis disappear again and he escapes alive, destined to live his life without Giselle.

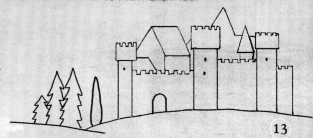

The Nutcracker

Setting: Germany, in the 19th century

The Nutcracker is a spectacular, Christmas-themed ballet that tells the story of Clara, a young girl who is given a special nutcracker in the shape of a soldier. Clara finds herself transported into a magical dream world where her toys come to life and her nutcracker turns into a prince. There are lots of fabulous characters, including the giant Mouse King and his army, the Snow Queen and her dancing snowflakes and, the sweetest characters of all, the Sugar Plum Fairy and Mother Ginger. Brimming with magic, this is one of the most dazzling of all ballets.

On Christmas Eve, the Stahlbaum family are holding a Christmas party. They decorate the beautiful Christmas tree, the guests arrive and all the children are given presents. Then the magician, Dr Drosselmeyer, arrives. He brings clockwork dolls that dance for everyone as he performs his mysterious magic tricks.

Dr Drosselmeyer gives Clara a nutcracker in the shape of a soldier. Her brother, Fritz, is jealous, even though he has been given his own present. He grabs the nutcracker from Clara and breaks it on purpose. Dr Drosselmeyer quickly mends the nutcracker, and it is then left under the Christmas tree while everyone goes to bed.

In the middle of the night, Clara goes downstairs, desperate to see her nutcracker again. The clock strikes midnight and suddenly everything becomes very strange – she is surrounded by giant mice! The nutcracker and an army of toy soldiers then magically come to life and fight a battle with the mice. The nutcracker is injured and the evil Mouse King nearly defeats him. To save him, Clara throws her slipper at the Mouse King, and the nutcracker wins the battle.

FIND THESE CHARACTERS OVER THE PAGE

Clara

The Nutcracker
Prince

Dr Drosselmeyer

The Mouse
King

The Snow
Queen

The Sugar
Plum Fairy

Mother
Ginger

The nutcracker is then magically transformed into a handsome prince, and Clara finds herself in the Land of Snow, surrounded by beautiful dancing snowflakes. The Nutcracker Prince dances with the Snow Queen and with the snowflakes. After the dancing, the Prince and Clara climb into a magical sleigh, which carries them away.

The Prince takes Clara through an enchanted forest to his home, the Land of Sweets. There are sweets absolutely everywhere – all kinds and all sizes! The Prince tells the Sugar Plum Fairy how Clara saved his life. Clara is given delicious sweets to eat and she sits on a gingerbread throne while watching lots of beautiful dances.

There are all sorts of dances to watch, including dances about chocolate and candy canes, dances about flowers, a dance by Mother Ginger and her children, who hide underneath her huge skirt, and a spectacular dance by the Sugar Plum Fairy herself. At the end, all the sweets dance together.

The Sugar Plum Fairy leads Clara and the Prince back to their sleigh, and kisses Clara goodbye. As the sleigh carries them away, Clara feels very tired and falls asleep. When she wakes up, she is back at home, lying under the Christmas tree. She looks down and sees her beloved nutcracker in her arms.

La Bayadère

Setting: India, long ago

Set in India, *La Bayadère* tells the story of Solor, a handsome warrior, and his love, Nikiya, a bayadère (temple dancer). Throughout the ballet, obstacles stand in the way of their love, as the High Brahmin (a priest) reveals his own love for Nikiya, and Solor is forced to marry someone else. With dagger fights, deadly snakebites and ghostly hauntings, this action-packed ballet is dramatic from start to end.

A great warrior called Solor returns from a hunt to join in with the Ritual of Fire at the temple. He hopes to see his secret love, Nikiya. The High Brahmin of the temple and his priests and temple dancers light the sacred fire. Nikiya, who is the best bayadère at the temple, dances for everyone.

The High Brahmin tells Nikiya that he loves her. She is not at all interested in his love and she rejects him. Later, she meets with her true love, Solor. They dance together and swear their love to each other over the sacred fire. The High Brahmin is furious that Nikiya likes Solor and not him.

In the royal palace, the Rajah (a king) decides that Solor would be a good husband for his daughter, Gamzatti. He shows Gamzatti a picture of Solor, and she falls in love with him. Solor is summoned to meet Gamzatti, and he is made to agree to the marriage, even though he is really in love with Nikiya.

FIND THESE CHARACTERS OVER THE PAGE

Solor

Nikiya

The High
Brahmin

The Rajah

Gamzatti

The Shades

Trying to cause trouble, the jealous High Brahmin tells the Rajah that Solor is in love with Nikiya. But instead of killing Solor, as the High Brahmin had hoped, the Rajah plans to kill Nikiya instead. In the meantime, Gamzatti tries to bribe Nikiya to leave Solor, but Nikiya refuses and is so angry that she attacks Gamzatti with a dagger. Gamzatti's ayah (a nursemaid) stops Nikiya just in time. Gamzatti swears that she will kill Nikiya.

To make matters worse, Nikiya is forced to dance at Solor and Gamzatti's engagement party. Gamzatti then tricks Nikiya by sending her a basket of flowers with a message that says they are from Solor. Nikiya is happy, until a deadly snake, hidden in the flowers, bites her. The High Brahmin offers her an antidote if she will marry him, but she refuses and dies.

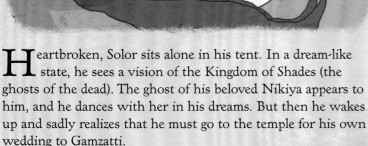

Heartbroken, Solor sits alone in his tent. In a dream-like state, he sees a vision of the Kingdom of Shades (the ghosts of the dead). The ghost of his beloved Nikiya appears to him, and he dances with her in his dreams. But then he wakes up and sadly realizes that he must go to the temple for his own wedding to Gamzatti.

At the temple, Nikiya's ghost continues to haunt Solor, and Gamzatti is annoyed that he seems unhappy and distracted. But the wedding ceremony carries on – until the gods get involved. They are angry because they know that Solor and Gamzatti aren't really in love. They destroy the temple and everyone in it. Solor and Nikiya are together again in death.

Coppélia

Setting: Poland, Eastern Europe, in the 18th century

Coppélia is a comic ballet that tells the tale of a beautiful, life-sized doll, built by a mysterious inventor called Dr Coppelius. The doll is so lifelike that a village boy, Franz, falls in love with it, forgetting about his own girlfriend, Swanhilde. The story is full of clever tricks and has characters hiding in cupboards, giving each other sleeping potions and dressing up in disguises. Luckily, the tricks work out for the best and the ballet ends with a happy wedding.

Every day, the beautiful Coppélia appears on a balcony above the house of Dr Coppelius, an old inventor. One day, sweethearts Franz and Swanhilde try to get Coppélia's attention, but she doesn't respond at all – she just sits completely still and reads her book. Meanwhile, the townspeople are getting ready for a festival to celebrate the arrival of a new town bell.

Swanhilde is jealous because she thinks that Franz is flirting with Coppélia by blowing her kisses. Swanhilde decides to test Franz's love for her by shaking an ear of wheat. According to an old tradition, if the wheat rattles, it means it's true love. Franz says that he can hear a rattle, but Swanhilde hears nothing and is heartbroken.

Later that afternoon, Dr Coppelius visits the local inn. While he is on his way there, he is pushed around by some boys and he drops his keys. Swanhilde finds the keys, and with some friends, sneaks into Dr Coppelius' house. Inside, they find a workshop full to the brim with amazing mechanical toys, including Coppélia, who they realize is really just a doll.

Dr Coppelius comes back from the inn. He angrily chases the girls out of the workshop, except for Swanhilde, who hides in a cupboard with Coppélia. Franz enters through the window, looking for Coppélia. Pretending to be friendly, the crafty Dr Coppelius offers Franz cups of wine, but he secretly adds a sleeping potion to the drinks. Franz falls into a deep sleep.

FIND THESE CHARACTERS OVER THE PAGE

Dr Coppelius

Swanhilde

Franz

Coppélia

The Mayor

Dr Coppelius wants to use Franz's life energy to bring Coppélia to life. But Swanhilde, who has been secretly watching from the cupboard, comes up with a clever plan. She puts on Coppélia's dress and pretends to be the mechanical doll. Completely delighted, Dr Coppelius thinks that his doll has really come to life. Swanhilde dances round the workshop wildly, causing havoc. Franz wakes up, and the couple escape.

Franz declares his love for Swanhilde, realizing how silly he has been. Swanhilde and Franz, and all the other engaged couples in the town, are to be married the next day in the Manor House garden. Dr Coppelius arrives and is angry about his damaged workshop. Swanhilde feels guilty about the mess she made, but the Mayor calms Dr Coppelius down by giving him a bag of money.

The next day, all the couples get married, and everyone has a party to celebrate the arrival of the beautiful new town bell. The bell-ringer plays the bells for the villagers, who perform dances based on the bell's different chimes: Morning, Prayer, Work and Marriage. Newly married and truly in love, Swanhilde and Franz dance happily together.

A Midsummer Night's Dream

Setting: Ancient Greece

Based on the Shakespeare play, *A Midsummer Night's Dream* is a comic ballet set in a magical forest at night. It's full of potions, fairies and funny mix-ups. Oberon, the Fairy King, wants to play a trick on his wife, Titania. He sends his servant, Puck, to fetch a love potion that will make Titania fall in love with the first person she sees when she opens her eyes. There are also four other people in the forest that night, and Puck uses the potion on some of them too, so you can imagine how confusing it gets!

In the forest near Athens, the Fairy King and the Fairy Queen, Oberon and Titania, argue about a baby boy they have stolen from the human world. Oberon sends Puck, his fairy servant, to fetch him the juice of a magical flower that makes people fall in love with the first person they see. As a trick, Oberon puts the potion on Titania's eyes as she sleeps.

Demetrius, a young man from Athens, is also in the forest that night. He is looking for Hermia, who he wants to marry. She has run away to the forest with her true love, Lysander. Helena, who loves Demetrius, is following him through the trees. Oberon tells Puck to use the magic potion on Demetrius to make him love Helena.

Meanwhile, deep in the forest, Hermia and Lysander lose each other. Seeing Lysander asleep, Puck gets confused and thinks he is Demetrius, so he puts the potion on his eyes. Lysander wakes up and falls in love with Helena, who happens to be walking past. Hermia is furious when she finds Lysander again, and sees that he is now in love with Helena and not her.

To add to the confusion, Puck then finds Demetrius and uses the potion on him too. He also falls in love with Helena and the two men fight over her. Puck magically sends everyone to sleep so that he can undo his mistakes. He casts a spell on Helena and Demetrius, and on Hermia and Lysander, so that when they wake up, they will love each other happily as couples.

FIND THESE CHARACTERS OVER THE PAGE

Oberon

Titania

Puck

Demetrius
and Helena

Lysander
and Hermia

Bottom the
weaver

Puck then finds a group of men rehearsing a play in the forest. Feeling mischievous, he casts a spell on one of them, Bottom the weaver, to turn his head into a donkey's head. When the sleeping Titania wakes up, she sees Bottom and, thanks to the magic flower potion, falls in love with him instantly. They perform a beautiful dance together.

In the morning, Duke Theseus of Athens and his bride-to-be, Hippolyta, visit the forest. They find the couples asleep, wake them up and take them back to Athens to marry each other at their own wedding later that day. Meanwhile, Oberon releases Titania from the spell, and Bottom is changed back to normal and allowed to go home.

Later that day in the city of Athens, at Duke Theseus' palace, there is a grand triple wedding for Theseus and Hippolyta, Demetrius and Helena, and Lysander and Hermia. There are wedding ceremonies, feasts and lots of dances, and the men perform their play. Back in the forest, Oberon and Titania make up and everything returns to normal.

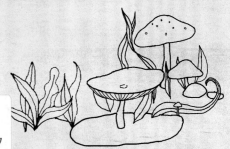

29

The Sleeping Beauty

Setting: A castle and a forest, long ago

The Sleeping Beauty is a classic ballet based on a much-loved fairy tale.
When Princess Aurora is born, her parents hold a christening party and invite lots
of good fairies from around the kingdom. However, they forget to invite the wicked fairy
Carabosse. Furious, Carabosse takes revenge by casting an evil spell on the baby Aurora.
Only one thing can break the spell – the loving kiss of a prince. Packed with both
kindness and cruelty, this ballet is all about true love saving the day in the end.

The King and Queen hold a christening party for their baby, Princess Aurora. But they forget to invite the wicked fairy Carabosse. In a rage, Carabosse gatecrashes the party and casts an evil spell on the baby Princess. The spell says that when Aurora turns 16, she will prick her finger and die.

As her gift to the baby, the kind Lilac Fairy changes the spell so that Aurora will not die, but will fall into a deep sleep instead. As Aurora grows up, the King and Queen try hard to make sure that there is nothing in the castle that she could prick her finger on.

Aurora's 16th birthday arrives and there is a huge party to celebrate. As the Princess and the guests enjoy the party, Carabosse sneaks into the castle in disguise, and gives Aurora a sharp knitting spindle as a birthday present. Aurora pricks her finger and falls into a deep, deep sleep. Just as Carabosse planned, the terrible curse has come true.

Desperate to help Aurora, the Lilac Fairy sends everyone else in the castle into a magical sleep as well, so that they will be with the Princess when she finally wakes up. The trouble is, the spell can only be broken by the kiss of a prince who is truly in love with her! A hundred years go by, and forests and thorn bushes grow up around the castle. Inside, everyone sleeps.

| Princess Aurora, as a baby | Princess Aurora, aged 16 | The King | The Queen | Carabosse | The Lilac Fairy | Prince Florimund |

One day, a prince called Florimund is out hunting when he gets lost in the forest. He is a lonely prince and all he wants is a wife to love. The Lilac Fairy appears and comes up with a clever plan. She shows him a vision of Princess Aurora and he falls madly in love with her at once. The kind fairy then shows him the way to the enchanted castle.

Fighting his way through the forests and thorn bushes to the silent castle, the Prince meets Carabosse. The wicked fairy tries to stop him, but he fights past her and makes it to the castle. He sees Aurora, the Sleeping Beauty, lying in her bed. Head over heels in love, the Prince kisses her and breaks the wicked spell. Straight away, everyone in the castle wakes up.

Aurora falls in love with Prince Florimund, and the King and Queen let them get married. In the end, there is a grand wedding, where other fairy-tale characters, such as Puss in Boots, and Little Red Riding Hood and the Wolf, dance alongside the Princess and her new husband.

Don Quixote

Don Quixote is a funny ballet based on a famous book. It follows the adventures of Don Quixote, a sleepy old man who has decided to become a brave and helpful knight, and his loyal sidekick, Sancho Panza. The comic pair set off on an adventure and end up trying to help two young lovers, Kitri and Basilio. After a series of silly escapades, including a fight with a windmill, Don Quixote becomes the hero that he always wanted to be and, thanks to him, the ballet ends happily.

While reading a book about knights and their adventures, old Don Quixote falls asleep in his study. He dreams that he is a brave knight, in love with a perfect, imaginary woman called Dulcinea. When his servant, Sancho Panza, wakes him up, Don Quixote decides that he wants to be a knight in real life, with Sancho Panza as his squire.

At an inn in the town, the innkeeper's daughter, Kitri, is in love with a local barber called Basilio. But the innkeeper, Lorenzo, does not like Basilio at all. He tells Kitri that she has to marry a nobleman called Gamache instead, who she hates. At this moment, Don Quixote and Sancho Panza arrive, looking for an adventure.

At first, Don Quixote thinks Kitri must be the beautiful Dulcinea of his dreams, and he dances with her. But then Kitri runs away with her true love, Basilio. Lorenzo and Gamache, along with Don Quixote and Sancho Panza, chase after them, and they all end up at a local camp.

FIND THESE CHARACTERS OVER THE PAGE

Don Quixote Sancho Panza Kitri Basilio Lorenzo Gamache

At the camp, Don Quixote and Sancho Panza are distracted from their adventure. They watch a puppet show, and Don Quixote now thinks that the female puppet must be his long-lost Dulcinea. He tries to save her from her puppet enemy. He then thinks a nearby windmill is a giant, and attacks it – before falling asleep again.

While asleep, Don Quixote dreams that he is a real knight, surrounded by beautiful women. The women include Kitri, who he again mixes up with Dulcinea. He is woken up by Lorenzo and Gamache, who want to keep following Kitri and Basilio. Don Quixote decides to help the lovers, so he leads Lorenzo and Gamache the wrong way to slow them down.

In the end, Lorenzo and Gamache find Kitri and Basilio. Lorenzo orders his daughter to marry Gamache. When Basilio hears this, he pretends to kill himself. With Don Quixote's help, Kitri persuades her father to let her marry Basilio's dead body before marrying Gamache. As soon as Lorenzo agrees, Basilio reveals he is really still alive!

Lorenzo and Gamache admit that they have been well and truly tricked, and Kitri is allowed to marry Basilio. The whole town celebrates the wedding with dancing, and Don Quixote is the guest of honour. Finally, he and Sancho Panza say goodbye to everyone, so that they can carry on with their adventures.

Cinderella

Cinderella is a classic ballet based on a famous fairy tale. Sweet and beautiful Cinderella lives with her father, stepmother and two stepsisters. Although loved by her father, Cinderella's stepmother and stepsisters are mean to her and make her do all the household chores. One day, a mysterious old woman comes to the house and something magical happens. Cinderella's life is changed forever – and it's in a good way!

Cinderella lives with her loving father, and her cruel stepmother and stepsisters, who treat her like a slave. They are excited about going to the ball at Prince Mikhail's palace, but Cinderella is not allowed to go. When a beggar woman comes to the house, the stepsisters rudely tell her to leave, but Cinderella is kind to her and lets her warm herself by the fire.

Cinderella's stepmother and stepsisters set off for the ball, leaving her alone. The beggar returns and reveals that she is actually Cinderella's fairy godmother. She gives her a beautiful dress and glass slippers, and she changes a pumpkin and some mice into a carriage and horses. Now Cinderella can go to the ball! But there's a catch – the magic will only last until midnight.

At the ball, Cinderella's stepsisters show off their terrible dance moves. Then Cinderella arrives. In her fairy carriage and her gorgeous dress, no one recognizes her, but Prince Mikhail asks her to dance straight away. As they dance, they fall deeply in love with each other. Everyone at the ball wonders who the mysterious new lady could be.

Cinderella is so busy dancing with the Prince that she forgets all about the time. The clock strikes midnight and she suddenly remembers what her fairy godmother told her. Afraid of her dress turning back into rags, and her carriage turning into a pumpkin, she runs away from the palace as fast as she can, leaving one of her glass slippers behind!

FIND THESE CHARACTERS OVER THE PAGE

Cinderella

Cinderella's father

Cinderella's stepmother

Cinderella's stepsister

Cinderella's stepsister

Prince Mikhail

Cinderella's fairy godmother

Back at home the next day, Cinderella wonders if everything that happened the night before was just a dream. But then she sees the other glass slipper and realizes it was all true. Suddenly, her father and stepmother come in looking very surprised and tell her that Prince Mikhail is about to arrive at their house.

The Prince walks in, holding the glass slipper that Cinderella left behind at the ball. He asks to see if the slipper will fit anyone who lives there. Cinderella's stepsisters demand to try it on first, but it doesn't fit them. Then her stepmother insists on trying it on. But, even with her two daughters pushing and pulling with all of their might, the shoe just doesn't fit.

Suddenly, the other glass slipper falls out of Cinderella's pocket and onto the floor. The Prince realizes who she is – the beautiful woman that he danced with all night at the ball. The fairy godmother appears and helps the couple to meet in secret. Prince Mikhail then asks Cinderella to marry him, and she says yes!

ANSWERS

Romeo and Juliet, 10–11

Coppélia, 26–27

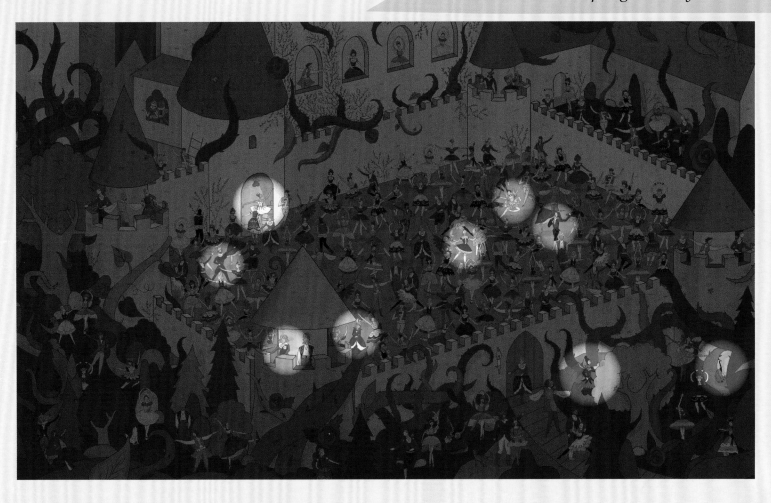